Simple Guidelines for Project Level PMO

Jay Jung

DEDICATION

For my family and friends who always prays for me.

CONTENTS

ACKNOWLEDGMENTS

This work could not have been completed on my own and I would like to express my sincere appreciation to those who gave countless supports and advices in writing this book.

To Niki and Evelyn, for their knowledgeable comments & valuable idea. To my dad, and other family members who in one way or another shared their support either mentally or emotionally.

Above all, to the Great Almighty God, for giving me experience, wisdom and knowledge to write this book, and of course, for His endless love and grace.

1 PMO-INTRODUCTION

1.1 Definition

PMO doesn't represent single abbreviation but it is an abbreviation of few titles.

Project Management Office (Division)
Project Management Officer (Individual)
Program Management Officer
Portfolio Management Officer

They are all correct. People use different title based on the extent they are executing their PMO job.

Regardless of their job scope, the essence of PMO is defining standard project process and monitor performance of projects to optimize success of project delivery and enhance overall project environment for the company.

"PMO is a Group/Individuals who defines the best project process and monitors adherence to the process to optimize project success rate."

1.2 History

History of PMO dates back to 1930s. U.S Air corps were developing an aircraft and unlike producing a simple product, there were numerous stream of works and they wanted to consolidate them under single management. This is when the term "Project Office" had first been introduced. In 1950s Project Office was implemented again in U.S military to develop complex missile system. This time it wasn't just about monitoring the work stream in a single view but also to apply phased execution approach with predefined standards. It wasn't until 50 years after the introduction of the term "Project Office" before it had been enforced to business industries.

In 1980s, concept of PMO was exported to construction and IT projects along with the boost of computer technology. Significant expansion of PMO function began after project management certification became recognized as industry standards. (E.g. PRINCE2, PMI PMP) Following figure summarizes history of PMO.

History of PMO

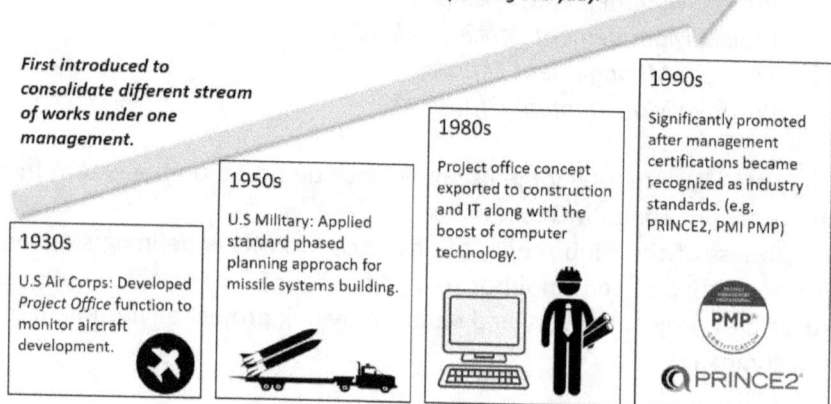

First introduced to consolidate different stream of works under one management.

Development of communication technology initiated PMO function in construction and IT industry. PMO function is evolving and expanding everyday.

1930s

U.S Air Corps: Developed *Project Office* function to monitor aircraft development.

1950s

U.S Military: Applied standard phased planning approach for missile systems building.

1980s

Project office concept exported to construction and IT along with the boost of computer technology.

1990s

Significantly promoted after management certifications became recognized as industry standards. (e.g. PRINCE2, PMI PMP)

PMP®

PRINCE2

1.3 Evolution of PMO Role

Responsibility of PMO had evolved over time from simple administration support to control over project prioritization to meet enterprise goal. Function of PMO began as an administrative support then modified to Project CoE (Center of Excellence) followed by Governance and Quality Assurance. Today, PMO plays key function in Corporate Strategic Alignment. For each stage of their role there were issues encountered and in order to overcome those challenges, PMO gradually developed their roles and responsibilities. Following table has detailed explanation of function performed and issues faced for each role. As you can see, there are still many challenges in today's PMO tasks and it is our job to continuously analyze and seek for better ways to guide project teams.

Evolution of PMO Roles

Main Duty	Roles Performed	Issues Faced
Administrative Support	· Act as a communication bridge to simply forward messages and reports. · Collect data and combine into single document. · Give reminder on important milestone.	· No authority to make decision or control project. · No standard process. · Considered as redundant communication layer and overhead count.
Project (CoE) Center of Excellence	· Define project process, templates to enforce best practice. · Facilitate post project review to enhance processes based on lessons learned. · Train and mentor project team on project management skills.	· Unable to track adherence to process. · Insufficient monitoring for quality assurance. · Recurred issues: Scope creep, unproductive use of resource, delay in decision making.
Governance / Quality Assurance	· Assign project level PMO to monitor and control project process. · Conduct quality assurance through project health check. · Create reporting system to collect data and provide sufficient input into decision making process.	· Projects does not always align to corporate strategic plan. · Projects are initiated without feasibility study. · Projects without clear objective are suspended.
Corporate Strategic Alignment	· Prioritize projects according to corporate business strategy and ensures investment in project provides the required business benefit. · Plan for best resource allocation to achieve long-term business goal.	· Still existing conflicts on prioritization approach. · People are resistant to changes and prefers to work without fixed standard process.

1.4 Challenges of PMO

Like any other jobs, there are several challenges faced by PMO. If you want to perform a good PMO role, you should expect to encounter following difficulties.

· **Resistance to change within the organization**
Regardless of how well the process is defined and how efficient it is going to make the whole job, people still prefer to stick to their own way of working. Standards, processes, policies are all considered as time consuming, redundant tasks distracting original work plan and shackling the team from free maneuvering of the project.

· **Value added by PMO is difficult to prove**
The ultimate purpose of having PMO function is to define process to improve project success rate and stakeholder satisfaction level. Unfortunately, this is not something we can measure in short term frame and even with clear indication of performance improvement, it is hard to determine exact portion of contribution that comes from PMO compared to the function with concrete deliverables.

· **PMO is perceived as overhead**
Due to difficulty in proving substantial value to the project, PMO is often perceived as unnecessary overhead count. This may also depend on company culture. Based on my experience, companies with distributed offices and global operation where standardized management is a must, tend to value PMO with high respect, whereas companies operating in one area with small organization treat PMO as redundant role.

· **Not enough time/resource for strategic activities to enhance existing process**
Defining a process that will bring the project performance to a whole new level requires long term analysis on past project success/failure data, bench marking models and market practices. It demands good amount of resources and investment to go from simple standardization to innovating corporate specific strategy. Unless PMOs put extra effort to study their project, it is easy to repeat same standard process over and over for all projects, which will not elevate efficiency or productivity.

· **Lack of knowledgebase to educate PMO skills**

There isn't enough knowledgebase to educate PMO skills relative to those that require specific skillset (E.g. Sales skill, programming, designing etc.). For companies without PMO function, it is difficult to even picture how PMO should be operating and this restrains official setup of PMO function, which is why I have decided to write this book!

· **PMO may not have high level of control over projects teams and functional divisions**

Depending on company culture, PMO may not have voice in the project. Without support from the management group, there will always be complaints and ignorance from the project team every time PMO steps in.

· **Global PMO is often regarded as a translator**

In global project environment, PMO is often considered as a translator. Project team expects no more than forwarding their messages and silently bury PMO's responsibility to monitor over adherence to the company process.

1.5 PM VS. PMO

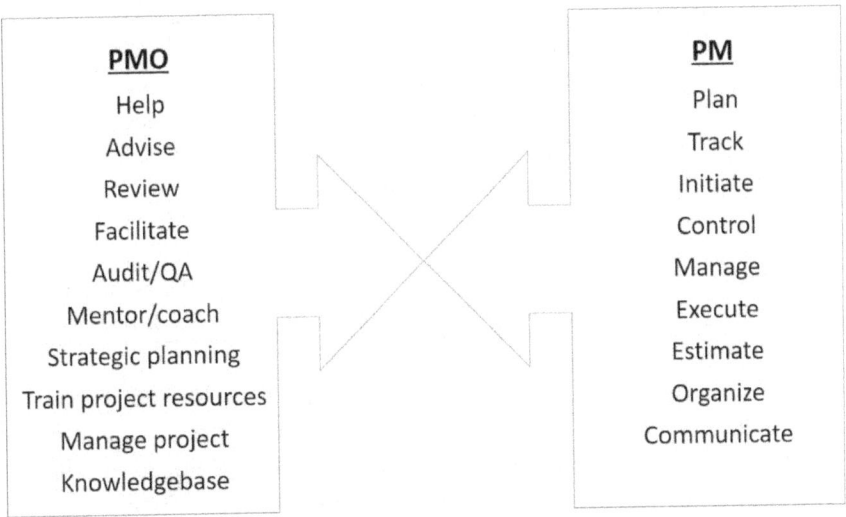

PMO	PM
Help	Plan
Advise	Track
Review	Initiate
Facilitate	Control
Audit/QA	Manage
Mentor/coach	Execute
Strategic planning	Estimate
Train project resources	Organize
Manage project	Communicate
Knowledgebase	

Many people ask difference between the role of PMO and PM in the project. Here are words that represents major role they perform. Of course, there are gray areas and you must note that roles being listed under PM, does not imply it is out of scope for PMO and vice versa.

PMO targets to implement process driven project environment and PM targets to achieve promised output for the project. It is clearly distinguished that PMO takes care of advising on standard process, review of overall task flow from the point of various stakeholders and mentor project team based on project management knowledgebase, whereas PM focuses on delivering promised output by planning, executing and estimating actual work progress.

Neither side is more beneficial, productive nor right than the other. They are both essential to achieve efficient and effective project environment. Detailed R&R of PMO and the project team in each project phase will be discussed in later chapters.

1.6 Influence to Project Management

Based on the influence and degree of control they have on projects within the organization, PMOs can be categorized as below:

Supportive	Supportive PMOs provide a consultative role to projects by supplying templates, best practices, training, access to information and lessons learned from other projects. This type of PMO serves as a project repository. The degree of control provided by the PMO is low.
Controlling	Controlling PMOs provide support and require compliance through various means. Compliance may involve adopting project management frameworks or methodologies, using specific templates, forms, and tools, or conformance to governance. The degree of control provided by the PMO is moderate.
Directive	Directive PMOs take control of projects by directly managing them. The degree of control provided by the PMO is high.

Executing supportive role in one project does not mean your company shall always consider PMO as a support group. Depending on the nature of the project, influence may vary and it is an important task for PMO to determine the best model for a given project. For example, a simple web site design change project that involves two engineers may not necessarily require directive PMO to close monitor programming process but rather support the team by providing company design guideline. In contrast, project with teams from five different cities will need strict management to tune communication between teams, making standardized reports etc.

1.7 Organizational Position

PMO can be categorized by their position in organization. All companies manage their business in portfolios, programs and projects. PMO managing portfolio level, program level, project level is called Corporate PMO, Departmental PMO and Individual PMO respectively. However, categorization of position does not mean a person can only be one of the three. Depending on the condition such as company size, project volume etc., a single person can perform multiple jobs.

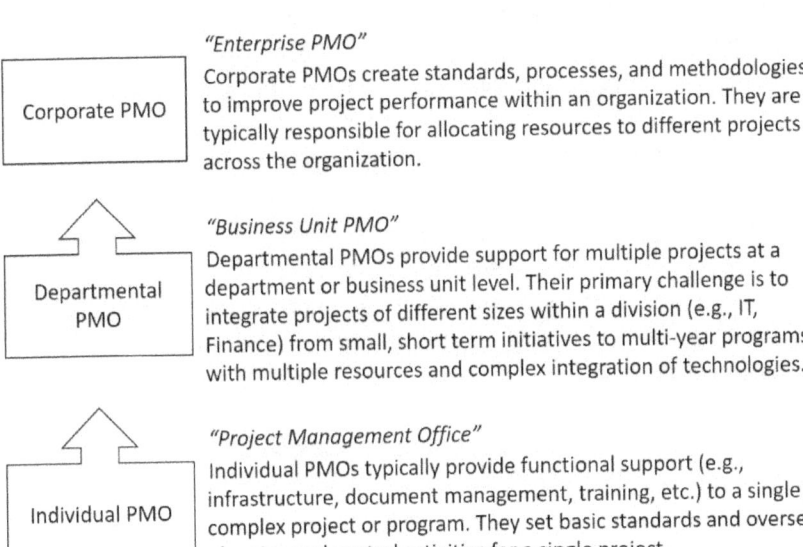

"Enterprise PMO"
Corporate PMOs create standards, processes, and methodologies to improve project performance within an organization. They are typically responsible for allocating resources to different projects across the organization.

"Business Unit PMO"
Departmental PMOs provide support for multiple projects at a department or business unit level. Their primary challenge is to integrate projects of different sizes within a division (e.g., IT, Finance) from small, short term initiatives to multi-year programs with multiple resources and complex integration of technologies.

"Project Management Office"
Individual PMOs typically provide functional support (e.g., infrastructure, document management, training, etc.) to a single complex project or program. They set basic standards and oversee planning and control activities for a single project.

1.8 Value of PMO

· **Repeatable project delivery process and less reinventing the wheel**
The most stable way to reduce risk of failure, minimize confusion and ease monitoring, is to have the project roll on the wheel that had been proven to be the best. In addition, if the process can be re-applied as a standard, then the cost of having to reinvent the wheel will no longer be consumed.

- **Continuous improvement of project culture, progress review towards completion and improved ROI (Return-on-investment)**

What succeeded in today's project environment may not always be the best remedy in the future. Company should continue to seek for improvement area and discard unproductive activities to optimize work efficiency. Project teams are often overloaded with tasks moving from one project to another without having enough time to review their course of work and there is no room for improving overall project culture. Analysis results and recommendations advised by PMO will promote flawless project execution flow, which will lead to greater ROI.

- **Accurate estimates based on firm's history and lessons learned**

One of the key success factors (KSF) to favorable project outcome is to plan it right in the first place. With PMO providing data on past project information and bench marking cases, project team is less prone to producing inappropriate project plan and repeating same mistakes.

- **Project priorities managed based on corporate strategic plan**

Although people in organization are all considered to be sailing in the same boat, it is not always the case when it comes to project prioritization. All projects are considered critical and urgent to the project owners and without PMO defining standard criteria for prioritization, company will be bombarded with business cases and endless arguments to win over budget.

- **Accurate resource management across projects**

Best resource planning can be achieved through consolidated monitoring of resource utilization. PMO enables allocation of resources based on their expertise rather than solely on their availability. Also by comparing planned and actual allocation rate, PMO may signal the team for safeguard.

- **Improved quality management**

One of the big interest and focus of Multi-National Companies is that they desire to leverage best practices from one country across the region for several purposes including cost savings, process standardization, quality maintenance and flexible management. In such projects, adherence to global guideline, policies and processes are compulsory. Consistent project management and guidance (methods, systems, processes, tools, metrics etc.) by PMO will enhance overall quality assurance.

· **Obtain senior management support and direction**

PMO are the professionals when it comes to executive reporting and communication. Delivering good quality output is one thing, making your project sponsor happy is another. Time to time, team needs support of senior management, and PMO is the key bridge to connect to management to speak for the team since they have good understanding of corporate strategic plan as well as the view point of project execution team.

2 PMO FUNCTION IN PROJECT MANAGEMENT

While project team focuses on execution of actual work to deliver output, PMO defines process and standards to improve efficiency, productivity, cost saving, stakeholder satisfaction level and probability of project success. PMO will provide appropriate guideline to the project team in each phase for managing changes, stakeholders, communication and reports. This book will run through process and standards required for the project based on each project phases.

Function of Project Team and PMO in the project

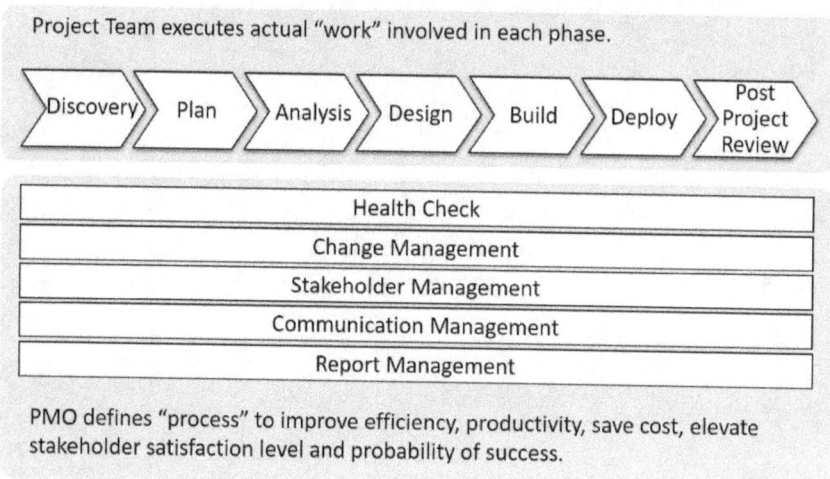

2.1 Challenges with Managing Multiple Projects

- Inaccurate scope definition and absence of detailed project plan to achieve defined scope.
- Lack of control on scope management.
- Lack visibility on resource demands and/or loads.
- Inability to review existing projects against changing priorities and conditions.
- No or irregular project health checks carried out.
- Inability to achieve on time on budget and quality of the deliverables due to lack of controls.
- Lack visibility on project procurement and/or contract management.

- Poor or no documentation and records management in place.
- Lack of risk management and consistency in quality.

2.2 Repeated Project Issues (That are never solved)

- Individuals complete their own task on time but we still face project delay in the process of integrating all work into a single piece.
- Project output is delivered on time and on budget, but there are still unhappy stakeholders.
- Often times deadlock occurs due to miscommunication, but no one attempts to make changes to existing process.
- People focus and put effort to meet deadline for tasks sitting on critical paths but not much committed in closing daily action items. (E.g. Answering questions, reviewing document, sending materials requested from their co-worker etc.)
- Clients/managers demand ad-hoc report which easily consumes half a day to produce.
- With absence of adequate communication plan, there are too many unnecessary meetings, calls and emails that makes it hard for individuals to make progress to their task.
- Some people just don't cooperate. They have a wall built around themselves which makes it difficult for other people to collaborate.
- No one keeps history of communication and action item completion status. In case of delay or confusion, it is hard to trace back where it started.
- Some people don't bother to discuss and resolve issues but sit on it until it becomes intolerable to handle by themselves, which most of the time is too late to be settled without impact to the project.
- There is no source of data which shows status of issues, pending items and upcoming deadlines in a single list with consistent update. Hence there is no common prioritization of task among the team.
- Project manager is too busy going around and tracking individual tasks. He/she is unable to identify where the project stands and see the big picture when it comes to decision making.
- All projects are different in volume, period, available resources, requirements etc. But they are forced to use same process which may not always be ideal. (E.g. Demanding 20 deliverables for a project less than 6 month is just too much.)

2.3 Why Define Project Lifecycle and Processes?

There are numerous projects being executed. Regardless of its purpose, tasks, outputs and resources involved, there are processes and standards that needs to be conformed in order to keep efficiency and productivity to the best.

"Project without defined life cycle/process is like driving a car with no lanes or signs. You may be able to reach your destination, but with intense risks and probability of failure!"

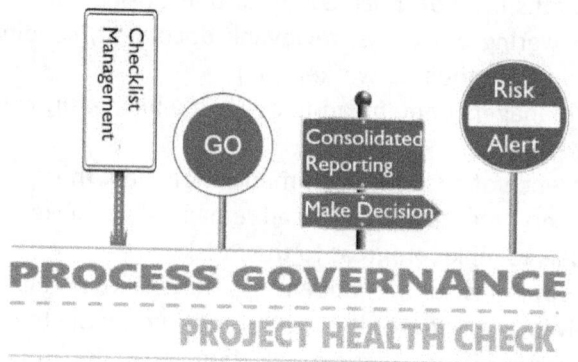

Ultimate goal of having a standard process is to convert project environment from unproductive and inefficient state to systematic and better manageable state. Commonly repeated problems listed in section 2.2 are mainly caused due to unstructured flow of work, inconsistent reporting and immature project execution environment.
Process aims to promote use of standard methodology and use of structured approach. Using repeatable processes and templates, maintaining consistent information and configurable workstream will upgrade maturity of the project team.

Entry/Exit Criteria

Having clear entry/exit criteria for each phase as part of process will harness the project from entering hazard. Early in the project, stakeholders decide what criteria will indicate whether the product or the system is ready for release which is referred as a standard for final approval. When we are dealing with short term projects less than 3 months, this should be fine. However, when it comes to large projects involving many sub parts throughout longer period, checking your deliverables only before the release is far too risky. And in case there is a missing or incompliant part, the cost of tracking down and solving the issue will be much higher. In order to avoid this chaos, we need to prepare and check entry/exit criteria for each end of major tasks. (i.e. for each end of Planning, Analysis, Design, Implementation, Test, Deployment phase)

Your job as a PMO is not to define entry/exit criteria by yourself, but to discuss with project team to determine 'must-check' items to move to the next phase. For example, project members in charge of web page design must obtain confirmation on color code and layout of the page. A tester in charge of stress testing must have all servers and automated tools ready before entering the Test Phase. PMO must discuss with the project manager and consult the right team member in order to list detailed entry/exit criteria. As project environment and conditions may vary throughout the phase, it is better to list high level checklist at the beginning of the project and revisit them to add details.

2.4 Benefit of Applying Standard Process

Benefit for employees

- **Enhanced ability to partner with clients through use of standard practices**

If you don't have a solid track to follow, it is often easy to lose control and become dragged by vigorous demands from your clients. Having a clear map will enable the project team to lead and navigate tasks.

- **Opportunity to leverage work within organization**

Processes may not always be followed in identical manner in all projects, but they can be used as a base to refine suitable process for the project which will make employee's job much easier.

- **Shortened learning curve by using standard tool sets and processes**

Use of standard processes will reduce time and cost consumed to learn how project should be executed every time employees are assigned to a new project. Employees can concentrate more on doing the actual work and make contribution.

· **Gaining of reusable skills for job rotation and career enhancement**
Repeated exercising of industry standard techniques and best practices will naturally strengthen professional skills which will elevate employees' utilization rate within organization and broader opportunities in their career path.

Benefit for clients

· **Improved probability of delivering products and services on-time**
Use of well-defined process with past success record will elevate chance of getting projects delivered according to the plan.

· **Acceleration of work accomplishments**
Having to-do tasks lined up as part of process will enable faster accomplishment of work since discussion on "What comes next?" will consume less of their time.

· **Improvement in product service quality**
Defined standards for output quality will avoid surprises caused by deliverables far below their expectation.

· **Reduction in risk by better planning and coordination**
Well planned processes such as decision making, risk observation, requirement change, phase gate reviews, deliverables review etc., will significantly reduce risk of project entering danger zone.

Benefit for organization

· **Enhanced monitoring through the use of standardized reporting**
Organization can keep track of all on-going projects through consolidated data and make the best use of resources and budgets to achieve corporate strategic goal.

· **Cost saving through reduction of suspended projects**

In every organization, there are considerable number of projects that are being suspended. Not only is this a waste of budget but will also deteriorate dedication of employees towards work. By preventing project initiation without clear purpose and monitoring of on-going project, will greatly reduce percentage of suspended projects.

- **Satisfied employees resulting in maximization of effort and increas ed dedication**

Assigning employees to projects suitable for individuals' expertise will not only develop project performance but also increase employee's satisfaction towards job. This will promote employee's ownership and determination to solve issues when project goes through difficulty.

- **Excellent reputation in industry**

Higher project success rate and professional ways of handling tasks by project teams will have the organization win excellent reputation in industry. Greater the reputation, the more business there will be for the organization.

In the following chapters, we will dive into what PMO function "literally" is responsible once the project is initiated.

3 DISCOVERY PHASE

The very first step before starting a project is to do a feasibility study to assess the project in various aspects. Discovery phase is an opportunity for business team to highlight needs to execute project and grant budget approval.

Entry Criteria	• Business needs identified. • Feasibility study team assigned.
Tasks for PMO	• Mentor/Support project team in creating business case by providing inputs from strategic perspective. • Provide requested information. (E.g. Internal/external approval submission, past project data.)
Tasks for Project Team	• Conduct feasibility study. • Create business case and make presentation for project approval.
Exit Criteria	• Resource commitment available. • Business case document. • Approvals from required parties. (Internal/External) • 1st round GO/NO GO decision.
Output Document	• Business Case. • Project approval signed by project sponsor.

- *Entry Criteria: Mandatory items to begin the given phase.*
- *Tasks for PMO: Works PMO will perform during the phase.*
- *Tasks for Project Team: Works project team will perform during the phase.*
- *Exit Criteria: Mandatory items that needs to be completed to get the phase signed off.*
- *Output Document: Documentations that should be produced besides the ones agreed with client as part of project deliverable.*

3.1 High Level Flow

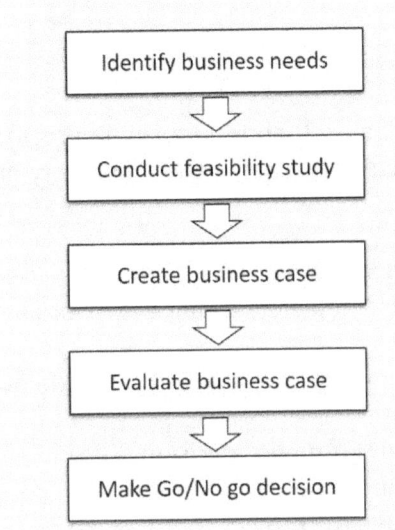

3.2 Consequence of NOT Conducting Discovery Phase

Projects fail not because of lack of skill, but lack of preparation. Here is a list of issues organizations encounter because they did not do proper feasibility study on the project.

- Some projects are executed with no clear benefit. (i.e. Executed for the sake of doing a project and using budget allocated.)
- Projects with obscure initiative easily derails from its original purpose.
- Project objective does not always align with company's strategic direction.
- Too many projects and too many voices make project prioritization difficult.
- Spending budget on unnecessary projects will block execution of important projects.
- Projects without good risk analysis will lead to project failure.
- Easily started projects are also easily abandoned without lessons learned. (i.e. Unproductive use of resource, repeated project suspension.)

- Projects started without much attention from managements will unchain project team's dedication to work.

3.3 Benefit of Conducting Feasibility Study

It is best to make determination in advance than to jump in and realize the project just won't work. Advantages of having a good discovery on the project includes:

- Improves project teams' focus and attention of management.
- Uncovers new ideas that could completely change the project scope. (i.e. New opportunities)
- Sets the end picture and assigns the right resource, time and cost from the start.
- Provides valuable information for a "go/no-go" decision.
- Reveals all possible solution and narrows down alternatives.
- Identifies a valid reason to undertake the project.
- Estimates return on investment. (ROI)
- Enhances the success rate by evaluating multiple parameters. (Risks, Constraints)
- Identifies reasons not to proceed.

3.4 Five Areas of Feasibility Study

Feasibility study is not just about doing a pre-study on what your team wishes to execute but it is also about convincing management to approve and agree on providing organizational support to execute the project. Your boss will not sign anything unless he/she is clear of benefits that company will achieve. So here are 5 areas that PMO should guide the team to focus during feasibility study.

Technical	• Determine technical resource capacity and the team's ability to convert ideas into working systems. • Evaluation of the hardware, software, tools, materials, equipment, skills and other technology requirements of the proposed project. • Explore alternatives that is more realistic and achievable.
Economical	• Assessment on cost/ benefits analysis of the project. • Determine viability, cost, and benefits associated with the project along with alignment with corporate strategic direction. • Enhance project credibility and help decision makers determine positive economic benefits to the organization.
Legal	• Investigation on whether any aspects of the proposed project conflicts with legal requirements. (E.g. Zoning laws, data protection acts, or social media laws.) • Determine legal obligation to conduct the project.
Operational	• Assessment on how well the organization's needs can be met by the project. • Determine alignment with company's strategic objective. • Evaluate operational risk and negative impact for not executing the project.
Scheduling	• Estimate how much time the project will take to complete. • Set high level timeline and milestone to be used as a guideline for detailing plans.

3.5 Contents of Business Case

Following table describes list of information that should be included in your business case. When you are writing a business case, you must keep bear in mind that your audience may not have enough understanding as you. Hence it must be written in a way any audience can comprehend.

Executive summary	Abstract of Current Issue/Expected Outcomes/ Approach/Justification.
Feasibility study team	Roles of the team members who developed the business case.
Problem definition	Business problem that this project was created to address. Problem may come from existing process, technology, or product/service etc.
Proposed project overview	Project description/Goals & objectives. Changes to organization. Assumptions. Risks and constraints. Major project millstone.
Project timeline	Provide information about the timeline for RFP (Request for Proposal) process as well as the project itself.
Strategic alignment	Provide an overview of the organizational strategic plans that are related to the project.
Cost benefit analysis (ROI)	Return on Investment over time. Costs or savings project will yield. It is important to quantify financial benefits of the project as much as possible in the business case as those will be the most convincing data for managements.
Alternative analysis	Brief summary of considered alternatives should also be included. Reasons for not selecting the alternatives should also be included.
Approvals	Approval authorities to move forward with execution of the project.

4 PROCUREMENT PHASE

Purpose of procurement phase is to select items that are required to deliver the project. Items can range from the contractor who will be in charge of executing the project to equipment, facilities, software etc.

Entry Criteria	Project Approved. High level project plan completed.
Tasks for PMO	Provide standard procurement process. (Bidding process, vendor due diligence, conformance to enterprise standard) Ensure procurement plan is lined up. Supervise process from vendor selection, contract review, cost negotiation.
Tasks for Project Team	Conduct bidding process. (Create RFP, Proposal, Presentation etc.) List and categorize items for buy, lease, reuse. Plan procurement. (material, equipment, supplies, machines, tools etc.) Prepare kickoff meeting.
Exit Criteria	Final contractor selected and announced. Final cost had been negotiated. Procurement schedules and purchase method. Contract terms and conditions agreed and signed by all relevant parties.
Output Document	Procurement Schedule. Signed contract.

4.1 High Level Process

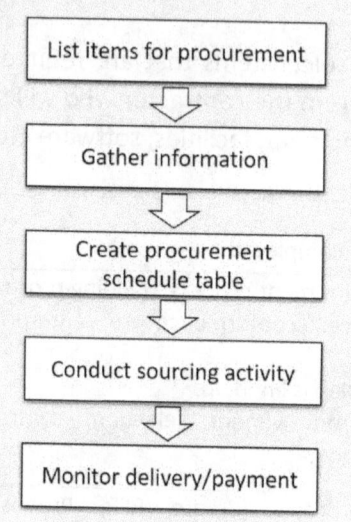

4.2 Important Guidelines

· **List items required including resources, equipment, system, faciliti es**

The very first step of procurement is to make a shopping list. You can identify procurement items by searching similar project records in the past, benchmark best practices in the market and consult subject matter experts. Always encourage the team to study new trends and practices in the market, so the team does not go for outdated procurement items.

· **Collect information on each item**

Collecting information about each item should follow as step 2. Don't be tempted to jump into buying products, but study specification, buying options and determine ballpark figure on quantity and cost. Most companies have approved vendor list managed by internal procurement team. Involving approved vendors will reduce risk and save time for corporate due diligence. However, project team should always stay open for other options that are more efficient and suitable for the project. You should also encourage the team to check availability of internal inventory.

- **Create procurement schedule table**

Procurement schedule table must be created and updated throughout the project. Buying option and schedule should be clear after studying each procurement item. Depending on company policy, budget allowance and project requirement, project team can either buy, lease, recycle or make a turnkey contract with service providers. It is important to determine lead time and prepare for procurement as required. More details on procurement schedule table is explained in next section.

- **Evaluate and select providers**

This is the step where we create request for proposal and distribute to candidate providers. Depending on the procurement item, you may request for a simple brochure, product samples or go through proposal review and vendor evaluation process.

Important point in this step is to set maximum number of people eligible for proposal evaluation and final vendor selection. Time to time, we are so focused in screening out candidate bidders that we don't pay much attention on trimming down proposal evaluation group. It is important to count on comments from all relevant teams but we can't spend our life trying to figure out the best way to satisfy hundreds of different voices. Also, sometimes people get involved in proposal scoring without much thought and this can blur inputs from people who has concrete reason for their scoring. Hence, you must limit number of people who will provide input in selecting final vendor. Have each team or department assign one or two people in charge of defining evaluation criteria and participating in proposal assessment. This way, we can be sure people from the same team will speak in one voice. Each team will also be much more considerate to assign a person who has high knowledge, interest, experience and influence to participate in procurement process on behalf of the team.

- **Engage contract and manage delivery/payment process.**

Last step of procurement is to engage contract based on procurement schedule, and continuously monitor and update procurement status for each item.

4.3 Contents of Request for Proposal

This is the general contents for request for proposal. It is recommended that project team uses standard template.

Summary/ Background	High level description of what the request for proposal is for and the purpose of the requirement.
Proposal guidelines	Description of what each responding organization's proposal should contain.
Project purpose and description	Purpose and description of the project or work to be performed in as much detail as possible.
Project scope	Details of what exactly is required for the project as well as what is not included as part of the project.
Project timeline	Information about the timeline for the RFP process as well as the project itself.
Budget	Explanation on what bidders should include in their proposals regarding cost estimation.
Bidder qualification	Description of criteria that will comprise successful bidder's organization. (E.g. Relevant project experience/accomplishments, contact information, company history, company size, organizational charts, or any other number of information to aid in the decision-making process.)
Proposal evaluation criteria	List of criteria that will be reviewed with detailed description on each criterion.
Appendix	Terminologies. Make sure you inform your organization specific terminologies so there is no risk of misunderstanding your requirement based on assumptions and dictionary meanings.

4.4 Procurement Schedule Table

Developing and maintaining a procurement schedule table is essential to manage commodity detail, contract status and timely billing/payments, especially for the projects with future purchases lined up throughout the journey. This is a simple table listing tracking details of each items. With big projects where several teams are involved, PMO must make sure everyone is using the same template with up-to-date information. For this, you will want to:

- Assign person in charge to update procurement status using standard template.
- Check on status during regular meeting for the items nearing scheduled event.
- Consolidate all items into master spreadsheet for management.
- Keep the table in company database as a reference for similar projects in the future.

Procurement Schedule Table Example

ITEM	IN CHARGE	PURCHASE METHOD	QUANTITY/ MAN HOURS	REQUIRED DELIVERY DATE	DELIVERY LOCATION	STATUS
Drilling Machine	Michael Cane	2 Years Lease	5	15th of Nov	Site A-1	Delivery complete
Vaccine Software	Jay Tang	Buy	20 licenses	5th of Sep	Data center	Delivery complete
TPC testing service	Tony Wong	Turnkey	100MM	1st of Mar	Site A-1	Under contract review
Painting Equipment	Jimmy Choi	Buy	50 packets	10th Nov	Site A-1	Pending

5 PLANNING PHASE

While the team is working on overall project plan, allocating tasks, defining high level scope etc., PMO should concentrate on how overall process of work should be done.

Entry Criteria	Contractor selected. Internal project team organized. Kickoff meeting preparation done.
Tasks for PMO	Guide in selecting project methodology. Confirm reports, documents that needs to be submitted for project monitoring. Provide templates for all necessary documents. (Deliverables, reports, trackers etc.) Identify stakeholders.
Tasks for Project Team	Conduct kickoff meeting. Estimate project cost and resource in detail. Prepare project plan. (Select methodology, Timeline, Org chart, communication plan, key stakeholder listing etc.)
Exit Criteria	Project team organized. Project kickoff completed. Project charter approved.
Output Document	Project charter. Project plan.

5.1 High Level Flow

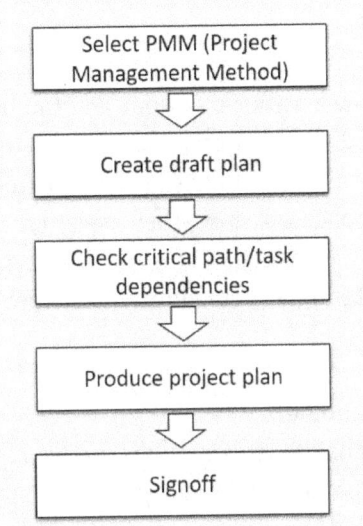

5.2 Key Activities for PMO in planning phase:

·   **Select Project Management Methodology (PMM)**

PMO must provide and guide the project team in choosing the right methodology.   Final decision should be made by the project team. However, PMO must be involved in discussion to prevent same PMM being practiced without reviewing suitability to the current project. Project Management Office must monitor performance of all projects and enhance PMM continuously to define productive way to execute a project.   Standardization of PMM is important but there should be options to choose from based on project characteristics. Standard PMM may vary depending on company standard.   Waterfall, Iterative, Incremental model are the three standards highly used in most industries.

·   **Confirm reports and other documents that needs to be submitted throughout the project**

Check all list of deliverables that should be submitted throughout the project. Important part of your job is to discuss and filter deliverables suitable and feasible for the project. Don't just agree to deliver 30-40 documents for a 6-month project.

· **Check document templates**

Find templates for each deliverable. Mark those without any template and make sure you discuss with the team and create one. For those with template, review them and discuss needs for adjustment. Standard templates are usually complicated since they were created with purpose to serve broad range of projects. You must trim non-mandatory parts and work with template customized for project requirement.

· **Identify and analyze project stakeholders**

It is crucial that you identify and analyze stakeholders early in the project. 'Stakeholder Management' process defined by PMI.org states that stakeholders must be classified according to their interest, influence and involvement for better relationship management by project managers. For PMO, you need to go a step further. As a center point of communication, you should also classify them into their involvement period, authority to view confidential data etc. It's no surprise that 10% of my inbox is filled with weekly status report from projects I have disembarked few months' past. I even had a PMO who zipped confidential cost estimation files from three different companies and circulated to the entire project group. Sounds like a silly mistake but people make this kind of mistakes and the worst part is they don't even know they have done so. Make sure you know who your stakeholders are and what to communicate with each group.

· **Create contact list**

Stakeholder contact information including name, email address, phone number, company name and R&R must be listed and shared with project group. For global projects where project team comes from different companies all over the world, it is also good to include country information so people have sense of a time zone when meetings are scheduled. This list should be regularly checked and updated throughout the project as there are members joining and leaving in the middle of journey.

6 ANALYSIS PHASE

In large scale projects where many sub-teams and parts are involved, risks are high due to vast requirements, distributed location, cultural gap, language barrier and unfamiliar policies/processes, which puts communication and collaboration much more difficult. It is too dangerous to assume that people will have same understanding when they leave the meeting room or when they sign off any document. The way each person understands the context may be different. It is crucial to have constant clarification on how things are being perceived and make necessary changes to remove gap among stakeholders and make sure requirements documented are consensual.

Entry Criteria	Project Plan signed off. Requirement preparation completed. (Template, gathering method etc.)
Task of PMO	Guide the team to conduct requirement gathering process according to company's standard.
Task of Project Team	Execute requirement gathering. Create document and manage updates. Review and provide feedback.
Exit Criteria	All requirements are confirmed and signed off by relevant stakeholders.
Output Document	Business Requirement Document. Requirement Traceability Matrix.

6.1 High Level Flow

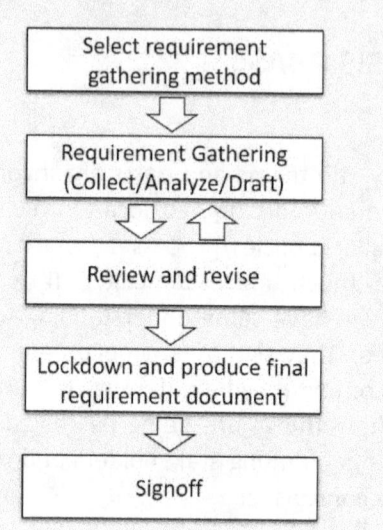

In preparing for requirement analysis, PMO must check if all minor/major things are ready and make the work flawless to avoid problems caused due to lack of preparation. Clients who are unwilling to cooperate and answers question with no more than a sentence is something we can't completely avoid. But if you are not being able to extract requirements in great detail due to disorganized questionnaire and inappropriate setting of analysis team, then this is due to lack of preparation.

6.2 Common Risks/Issues in Requirement Gathering

Category	Behavior of Issue
Inappropriate Approach	• Project teams have strong tendency to repeat past project experience. • Only 'gather requirement' without 'review, analysis and confirmation'. • Involving inappropriate stakeholders. • Excluding critical stakeholders/consumers.
Lack of Collaboration	• Project team expects client to know all the requirements. • Client expects project team to recognize unconscious requirements.

	• People don't know what they want. • People only focus on what they want. • People choose to surrender than to discuss. • People don't give clear comment or confirmation.
Poor Documentation	• Too much verbal communication but lack of record. (Remember! What is not documented is considered to have never been said.) • Documents are not detailed down to traceable level. (Not useful in design phase.) • No standard format. (i.e. Difficult to document, difficult to understand.) • Documents are out dated after few rounds of discussion.

6.3 Solution

Category	Solution Description
Inappropriate Approach	• Select requirement analysis approach based on "current" project environment. • Make sure to prepare the right environment for selected approach.
Lack of Collaboration	• Routinize requirement review and analysis session. • Set clear policy on change requirement after signoff. • Make recommendation based on supporting facts.
Poor Documentation	• Define standard template for requirement document. • Provide good training on how to use the template. • Assign person in charge to review and confirm each section.

6.4 Requirement Gathering Process

·   Preparation

PMO should prepare to setup the environment for analysis phase while the team focuses on project planning. You will need to discuss with project manager and list mandatory items that should be in place to begin next phase. Do not hold this task until the end and rush in with only few days remaining before analysis phase begins. It could force entire team on hold.

1) Decide requirement gathering approach.
2) Define detailed process for selected approach, set policies.

3) List down things required for requirement gathering. (E.g. Meeting environment setup, site investigation, required engagement from users, access to current system, bench marking model tour, questionnaire for user interview etc.)

Example: Requirement Gathering Preparation List

Gathering Method	What is required
Business User Interview	- Meeting with sales support team. - Expected Duration: 2 weeks full day onsite workshop. (Mon-Fri 10am-6pm, Jakarta HQ Office)
Sales Agency Tour	Agency tour for business hour operation analysis. - 10 selected agencies with top 5/bottom 5 sales performance.

4) Create timetable for EACH day. (Start time, location, duration, participants, agenda, expected output, Daily wrap-up schedule.)
5) List contacts for all participants.
6) Define templates for requirement drafting.
7) Train the project team on process and how to use the template.

· **Requirement gathering tips**

✓ Start on time, have participants located where they should be.
✓ Distribute agenda in advance so nobody comes in or leaves empty handed.
✓ Clients will NOT tell you what you don't ask. (Scrutinize rather than just collect)
✓ Clarify even the obvious items and avoid unconscious requirements.
✓ Collect both functional and non-functional requirements.
✓ Conduct daily end of day wrap-up to review percentage of progress for the day's plan, discuss summary of observation and analysis, issues faced during session (E.g. Absence of user, passive attitude, system access issue etc.), check conformity to template and alert possible changes to existing plan.

· **Requirement Gathering Template**

Many people, in fact almost everyone, put a lot of effort and time into requirement gathering, but never put them into proper documentation unless instructed to do so. Most would say it is all in their notes and brain, they've settled everything during the interview and they know what to do, and when I request them to put them into a document, they would just send me list of notes they had jotted down.

One of our goal as a PMO is to accelerate communication but still make it clear and stable by finding and encouraging smart ways to document things. Here are some tips.

- Use of spread sheet is strongly recommended to divide requirements into category.
- Break down 1st level category into sub-categories to state detailed requirement.
- Use short and easy description.
- Prepare high level category/sub category section before analysis session. This can be used as a starting point for detailing.

Example: Requirement Gathering Preparation List

ID	Category	Sub-Category (Function)	As-is	To-be
1	Building Interior	Lobby floor plan	Refer to floor plan specification 2.4.1	Elevator location: Main Entrance:
2	Building Interior	Typical floor plan	Refer to floor plan specification 2.4.1	Stairway exit door:
3	Access Control	Building entrance	Employee card scan	Finger print scan
4	Building Exterior	Access from main road	...	...
5	Network	Internet connection	Only available in lobby LAN line used in other floors	Provide Wi-Fi connection in entire building

It is important that requirement document is continuously monitored to pre-detect items that could make requirement document being rejected for re-work. PMO must ensure documentation is detailed and clear enough to be used as a reference any time there are questions, conflicts and changes.

- **Requirement Traceability Matric (RTM)**

Requirement Traceability Matrix (RTM) is used throughout the life of project to ensure success of the project by having an end-to-end traceability. Starting from breakdown of requirement, each item is coupled with design, implementation, testing document section ID to guarantee delivery of all collected requirements. RTM must be updated and confirmed at the end of every project phase.

Example: Requirement Traceability Matrix

Business Requirements Document Section	Requirement Keywords/ Description	Design Document	Unit Test Cases	UAT Test Cases
1.1	Building Floor Plan			
	Room Size			
	Hallway interior			
1.2	Security system			
	Employee access card			
	Alarm system			

- **Review and Signoff**

Project team should:
- Setup a session for feedback discussion, so people will be more responsible about the review.
- Request review on drafted requirement so changes can be applied to the final one.

Client team should:
- Never make assumption. Raise question for any unclear parts.
- Give confirmation if there is no issue. Do not wait until the last day.
- Be open to alternative options. Do not be too dominant or too submissive.

- Make timely update on document. Do not expect anyone to remember.

Once the requirement is finalized, lock them down in Business Requirement Document and Requirement Traceability Matrix and have documents signed off by key stakeholders who actually provided the input.

7 DESIGN PHASE

Design phase is executed after requirement document is finalized and approved by relevant stakeholders. Before starting the actual design work, PMO must check for any design guideline policy and share it with the project team. Promoting regular design review session is also critical to avoid scope creep and discrepancy between final design and the actual requirement.

Entry Criteria	Project Plan baselined. BRD approved and signed off.
Task of PMO	Guide project team to conduct regular design review. Provide policy/guideline on requirement change request. (CR)
Task of Project Team	Create design document based on BRD. Execute design review session. Manage requirement change request.
Exit Criteria	Design document approved. Risk evaluation done and confirmed.
Output Document	Design Specification Document. Updated RTM. (Requirement Traceability Matrix)

7.1 High Level Flow

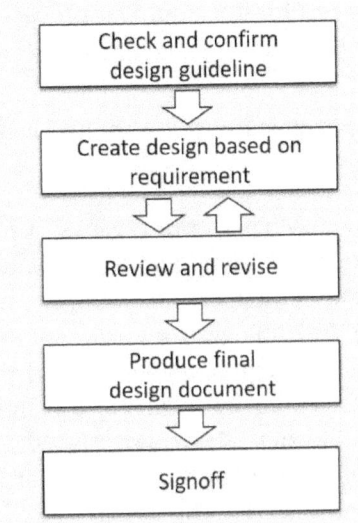

7.2 Interim Design Review

Imagine you are renovating your old house. Even if you already know what materials will be used and how the place will be renovated, you would still expect the architect to show you a sketch of what it will roughly look like. In the project, you should guide the team to have interim review session with stakeholders in charge of approval when certain portion of design is complete enough to show the frame of the output. (E.g. Menu navigation flow of new mobile application, floor plans of renovated building etc.) Depending on the size of project and duration of design phase, you may have to schedule sessions more than once. For a project with 2-weeks of design period, quick walkthrough during weekly meeting could be enough, whereas for a project with 6 months of design period may require couple of sessions divided by functions.

Benefits of Interim Design Review

- This will avoid surprises and major changes to completed design at the end of the phase.
- Consistent review of design will save time for approval process as certain portion of design work had already been agreed and confirmed.
- Cost of making changes in design phase is much lower than it is in implementation phase.

Although clients are happy with idea of having interim reviews, it may not always be the same for project execution team. Some people take it as clients inspecting their work because they are not being trusted enough, some just don't want to spend time doing extra documentation and some people, especially the project managers, are concerned that flow and rhythm of work could be interfered by receiving too many comments from clients, which is partially true. There are clients who come back with 100 comments mostly demanding for minor changes which will definitely put a stop to ongoing work. The whole idea is to review overall shape of final output and advise on items discrepant to requirement. PMO should emphasize this rule at the beginning of the session.

7.3 Managing Requirement Changes

Requirements change during design phase due to many reasons. If requirement change is not properly managed and documented, this will all lead to scope creep. Changes include:

- Changes to business requirements.
- Changes to agreed and approved architectural and technical decisions or work products.
- Changes to list of deliverables.
- Changes to project commitments. (such as milestone, costs, budgets, timelines)

Requirement changes are inevitable due to following reasons:

- Users change requirements without considering impact on time and cost of project.
- People neglect to confirm on clear explanation/understanding in the first place. (i.e. Team did not follow analysis phase process properly)

- Ambiguous wordings can set different perceptions to different individuals.
- There are costs and efforts that can only be identified in the process of putting words into design.
- Some requirements may sound reasonable but impossible to logically fit into the big picture.

Good news for PMO is that you don't have to figure out which requirement change requests to agree or disagree, how it will impact the project time, cost and resources, and do the re-planning accordingly. That's Project Manager's responsibility.

Your task as a PMO is to provide your PM and the team with clear and organized information on change requirement so they can use your data to discuss, negotiate and reproduce plan if necessary. The keyword here is 'organized'. You can't just circulate merged list of requirements and expect the team to filter out requirement gap. Remember! You are in the team to make the whole flow of work more efficient and so help the team to focus on what they need to focus to get the wheel moving.

Here is how you should guide the project team to manage requirement change request:

1) Project team must keep track of requirements newly brought up or modified during design review session. Instruct the team to mark any new or changed requirement and enter 'Y' for item with impact to project and 'N' for minor item that can be changed without changes to project plan.

ITEM	DESCRIPTION	CHANGE OR NEW REQUIREMENT	IMPACT TO PROJECT (Y/N)
1	Color of roof: Red	Change	N
2	Shape of window to be changed from Round to Rectangle	New	Y

2) Extract items with impact to the project and have the project team discuss with client on items that can be left out of scope. For

unnegotiable items, open steering committee meeting to make final decision.

If there are too many modified or new requirements, it is a sign that communication is not being done sufficiently. PMO must address this issue strongly and have the senior management reinforce the team to execute tasks with appropriate communication and process.

7.4 Use of Standard Design Document Template and Updating RTM

Final design document must be submitted and reviewed by relevant stakeholders. In most projects, documentation is not done by a single person but by many different teams and it is important for PMO to ensure adherence to standard templates. Many times, review and approval process are delayed due to irregularity of submitted deliverables. Also, as the project proceeds to implementation phase, design team must transfer all design documents for implementation team to use as instruction for the build. Hence it is crucial that design document is in consistent format, uses standard terminologies and documents similar level of detail.

Another significant area of focus would be to update the RTM discussed in section 6.4. As mentioned earlier, RTM links every single requirement to design, implementation and test. Design document ID and section should be mapped with respective requirement to make certain there are no omitted requirements or design work done for unconfirmed requirement. (i.e. Scope creep)

Final document must be submitted with consideration for review period. Do NOT submit everything in last minute knowing that stakeholders will not have enough time for review and commenting.

8 IMPLEMENTATION PHASE

What should be delivered and how it will be delivered are discussed and approved in analysis phase and design phase respectively. In implementation phase, project team will start building the actual product based on output from previous phases.

Entry Criteria	Design specification signed off. Build environment ready.
Task of PMO	Monitor resource and cost usage, progress. Conduct random project health check. Provide policy/guideline on stakeholder management. End of phase checkpoint review.
Task of Project Team	Execute implementation/build based on design specification. Manage requirement change request. Create test plan/test case document.
Exit Criteria	Test case reviewed and approved. All build work completed based on design document.
Output Document	Test plan/test case. Updated RTM. (Requirement Traceability Matrix)

8.1 High Level Flow

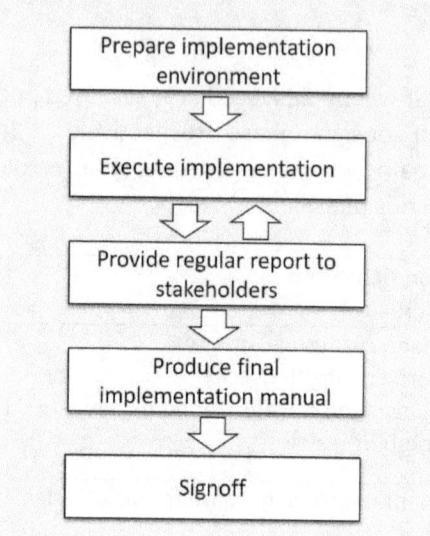

8.2 Interaction with Stakeholders in Implementation Phase

In general, highest portion of time, resource and budget is spent during implementation phase. But in contrast, the level of engagement from client is the lowest.

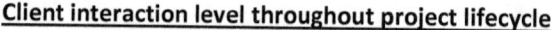

Client interaction level throughout project lifecycle

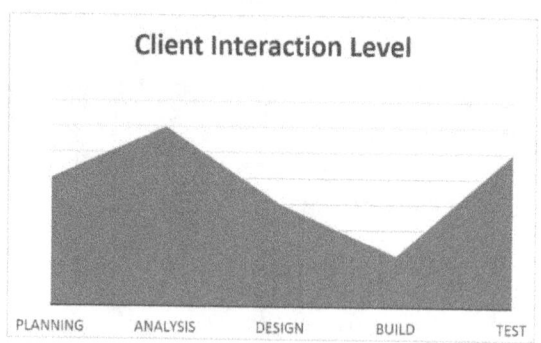

Many people assume daily report and weekly meeting will be enough to keep the stakeholders satisfied. You must bear in mind that most stakeholders can't afford to fully dedicate themselves to the project.

Business team has BAU (business-as-usual) tasks to handle and senior executives are looking after vast number of projects. Hence, they can't afford to keep track on your progress report. They may not even know what information they should be looking for. Stakeholders expect the team to provide indication that the wheel is moving as planned and project is located where it should be.

On the other hand, implementation phase is where the project team is most occupied. They are overwhelmed by implementation tasks and the last thing they would accept on their to-do list is having to pamper stakeholders on their inquiries. Project team expects stakeholders to be just as aware about the project as they are through regular reports and meetings. And if there is anything stakeholders want to know, they should search through deliverables submitted.

Both the stakeholders and the project team have their point. It is obvious that stakeholders want sense of comfort through continuous feeding of information and at the same time, project team can't interrupt main stream of task to deal with endless inquiries. This is where stakeholder management becomes crucial.

8.3 Stakeholder management overview

Stakeholders are people, group, organization that could be impacted by or have impact on the task outcomes throughout the project lifecycle. Success of the project is significantly bound to stakeholders as they may have strong influence to the work and power to assess the outcome of the project. The range of stakeholders is much broader than what we can determine from the project organization chart and project team may not even be aware of stakeholders with no direct interaction. Involvement of stakeholders may range from occasional participation on simple surveys to full project sponsorship.

What makes the project more complicated than it is from the load of the work, is that the stakeholder satisfaction cannot be fulfilled simply by meeting the scope, schedule and budget. While your end users will give you A+ for their renovated office, the building operation team may rate your work D- for creating noise and dust during renovation period. In the past there was less competition to win over projects and the only voice that was important was the voice of end users. Nowadays technology and skills are available everywhere and competition is shooting up sky high. Companies are being assessed not only by the output of their work but by the performance during their journey as well, and comments from every relevant stakeholder counts. Yes, you have eyes and ears everywhere.

8.4 Stakeholder Management Process

Stakeholder groups include (but are not limited to):
· Program Manager
· Functional Manager
· Operational Manager
· Customers
· Governments
· Business Partners

Stakeholder management process is divided into three main stages. Identify, Plan and Manage. It is not a single event during planning stage but should be repeated throughout the project as stakeholders' status (influence, interest, expectations etc.) vary at different stages of the project. Following table details about stakeholder must be collected and revised regularly as the project journey proceeds.

Information Type	Attributes
Identification	Name, organizational position, location, role in the project, contact.
Assessment	Requirement/Expectation, potential influence, phase of the project with the most interest.
Stakeholder Classification	Internal/External, Unaware/Resistant/Neutral/Supporter/Leading.

Step 1 > Stakeholder Identification

· Purpose of this stage is to find and list individual, group, organization with any possible relation to the project.
· Output: Long list of potential stakeholders.
· Stakeholder identification MUST commence from discovery phase.
  i. Define key stakeholders first. It is easy to define key stakeholders, hence should be the starting point. Anyone in decision making

group or management with direct impact from the project outcome are considered as key stakeholders. (i.e. Project sponsor, Project manager, Primary customer.)

ii. Interview key stakeholders and expand your list.

iii. Study and research similar projects in the past. Consult subject matter experts, project managers with similar project experience. Review past project data to see categories of stakeholders.

Step 2 > Stakeholder Analysis

- Purpose of this stage is to analyze your stakeholders and plan approach to manage them.
- Output: Stakeholder register.
- Key consideration points for stakeholder analysis:
  - Interest – What is the level of interest they have towards the impact of the project? (L, M, H)
  - Influence – What is the level of power they hold over the project (L, M, H)
  - Expectation - What is important to the them?
  - Support Action - How could they contribute to the project?
  - Resistant Action - How could they block the project?
  - Engagement Period – In which phases do they have the strongest binding?
  - Engagement Strategy – How shall we communication with them to avoid resistant and get support?

Example: Stakeholder Register

I=Interest, P=Power

Name	Contact	I	P	Expectation	Engaged Period	Support Action	Resistant Action	Engagement Strategy
Environment Protection Institution	Email Phone	H	H	Compliance with environmental protection regulation	All	Provide updated information on environment friendly assessment criteria	Disapproval on/Delay on environment friendly assessment	-Communicate on critical assessment items from early stage of the project -Conduct site inspection quarterly
Audit team	Email Phone	L	M	Non violated financial transaction against internal policy and contract	Adhoc	Grant green light and waiver on further audits	Report negative statements on disregarding internal policy	Involve audit team for critical processes (e.g. contract review, financial transaction etc.)
Local Residence Community	Email Phone	H	H	No disruption (noise, dust etc.) Compensation on disruption	Initiation/ Construction	-Not filing complaints -Building positive perspective	Filing official complaint on disruption caused by site work	-Open conference to present future benefits to local area -Conduct meeting with key members to acknowledge their concerns and complaints
Procurement Team	Email Phone	L	L	Prefers to work with vendors already in company procurement list	Procurement	Conduct procurement activities as planned	Reluctant to consume time and effort to run due diligence on new vendors	Provide good information on engaging contract with vendors selected

46

Step 3 > Stakeholder Management

- Purpose of this stage is to monitor status of key stakeholders at a given period and conduct necessary communication to keep engagement level at a desired status.
- Output: Stakeholder status monitoring matrix, update on stakeholder register
- Detailed communication plan must be produced based on various factors such as stakeholder's location, relationship with the project team, availability, policy etc.
- Monitoring and updating of stakeholder status is crucial as it will vary based on the progress and status of the project.

8.5 Key Advises PMO Must Provide to the Project Team

- Update stakeholder register and categorization for each phase.
- Inform customized information. Do NOT send 50page document to entire stakeholders all the time.
- Never treat stakeholders on negative side as an outsider and abort them from information loop.
- Leverage stakeholders with positive attitude to create active atmosphere to stakeholders with negative view.
- Keep close monitoring on negative stakeholders to inform them with appropriate information.

9 TEST PHASE

In test phase, we validate if implementation is done in a correct way. Test cases are created in two parts. One, functional test cases to verify operation of required function and two, non-functional test cases to examine level of performance for each function. What is important for PMO is to analyze implication of test progress and signal red flag if there is a risk of delay.

Entry Criteria	Test plan and schedule. Test environment ready. Test progress review communication plan.
Tasks for PMO	Analyze and identify test phase status. Provide input for decision making on approval to move to next phase.
Tasks for Project Team	Execute test. Fix issues. Execute test result review session.
Exit Criteria	All test completed. Transition plan prepared.
Output Document	Test case signoff document. Transition Plan.

9.1 High Level Flow

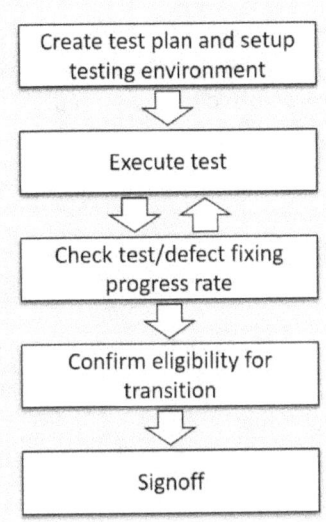

9.2 Frequent Issues During Testing

Criteria	Issue	Solution
Misjudgment on current status	• People often judge test status based on progress percentage only. • Project team often loses track of current status and just struggle to fix defects without prioritization. • It is easy to focus on quantity of defects fixed rather than quality of fixes. This will lead to recurring defects.	• Identify overall trend, inform detailed status and provide necessary data to establish issue fixing plan. • Track not only the number of defects fixed but percentage of reopen rate to assess quality of fixes.
Insufficient test cases	• Test cases are prepared in too high level. • Test progress is measured based on different standard	• Guide project team to agree on granularity of test cases. • Assign test manager to

	for each team. ・Test runs with no planned cases. Difficult to estimate schedule/resources required. ・Test cases are not evenly distributed to testers. (i.e. Too many overlapping issues, too many non-tested items.)	review and approve on final test case. ・Have key members signoff on final test case document to avoid scope creep.
Inadequate defect report	・Unclear steps to reproduce the defect. ・Some defects need fix/no fix decision. ・Minor change requests may slip into defect list. (i.e. Scope creep)	・Set regular defect review session to discuss unclear items.
Risk measuremen t	・Unexpected crisis. (E.g. Shut down of technical system, severe weather, complaints from parties with impact to their daily business etc.)	・Guide project team to prepare contingency plan. (i.e. Alternative option to run test, flexibility to switch schedule etc.)
Lack of test skills	・Users consume longer time to test than expected. ・People have different standard to grade defect severity. ・Some testers neglect logging defects into the system.	・Provide training session for: -Instruction on how to test. -Logging test result. -Grading defect. (S1=Severe, S2=Major, S3=Minor, S4=Cosmetic) -Writing steps to reproduce defect.

Inadequate environment setup	• Inadequate test environment slows down testing process. • Not enough dedicated resources for testing.	• Ensure project team is aware of lead time to prepare required items for test environment and begin preparation accordingly.

9.3 Test Phase Preparation Checklist

Thorough preparation is the number one key to successful execution of test phase. Even if the output from implementation is error-free, if it cannot be verified in flawless manner, there will be delay to the schedule. We don't want to jeopardize hard work done in implementation phase by neglecting to check on mandatory items required for testing. Below table lists sample checklist.

Test Phase Checklist
Test cases are listed based on Requirement Traceability Matrix.
Test group organization plan. (Unit, integration, user acceptance testing, non-functional testing e.g. stress/security/resistance testing etc.)
Defect registration tool/spreadsheet readiness.
Test progress review plan. (Report template, regular meeting schedule, communication method)
Define standard for severity(s1~s4) level.
▪ Test environment readiness: Test environment/equipment/site availability. (Right capacity) Automated testing tool/system readiness. Access granted for required systems, sites, information. Check impact to other on-going work.
▪ Overall schedule and process: Test by user group/by product/by functions. (Parallel, sequential etc.) Regular release schedule, release note template.
▪ Training: How to use test defect registration tool/report template. Provide user manual and train how to use system/equipment. Inform standard for severity/priority.

9.4 Defect Review Session

Jay Jung

PMO must guide the project team to conduct regular defect review session. Frequency of meeting should be based on the time window to conduct the test and retrieve result. For example, you might want to do a daily review session for mobile device functional testing since most test results can be observed on the spot and many test cases can be verified on daily base. On the other hand, if you are running a test for new cosmetics, it will take much longer than just a day to verify reaction of chemicals to human cells. Often times people repeat their past practice and plan for defect review session as they did in their previous projects. It is important for PMO to advise the team to determine frequency and grouping of defect review session with testing group based on testing environment. However, in no circumstances, should the team leave out this session and solely depend on documented result.

Tips for conducting defect review session

Instruct communication plan	Focus on following factors	Monitor session
• Register defects according to agreed format/detail. • Submit report by agreed time. (E.g. 3pm HKT Daily) • Inform meeting time & conference info. (E.g. 4pm HKT Daily, Bridge code: #156609)	• Unreasonable delay in testing/fixing. • Issues that cannot be reproduced/observed by project team. • Defect Vs. Change Request. • Review severity of defect. • Aging of defects. • Reprioritize test cases to avoid time wasted in functions yet to be fixed.	• Avoid personal attack. • Prevent dragging of call on single defect. • Discuss and make judgement based on original test plan. • Alert project team for change of project status.

9.5 Test Result Data List

Summary of test progress must be collected and updated until all issues are closed. Following are list of data that needs to be managed.

Data	Description
Test Execution Rate	Plan. VS Actual.
Defect Status	Number of defects for each category. (Severity/Priority)
Defect Burn Rate	How fast the team is fixing. (# of fixes VS. # of new defects)
Defect Reopen Rate	Impact of fix to other areas.

Let's go through what each data can tell us about our test progress and what are the things PMO must highlight to the team.

Test Execution Rate

This data indicates how well the testers are doing. The speed of testing may fluctuate based on scenario of test cases, but PMO should still keep sense of average number of test to be conducted and make sure to put up a warning light in case the gap is too big. Following are the questions PMO should be addressing to the team.

Progress Status	Things to Consider
Planned is higher than Actual	What is making delay? · Environmental issue. (E.g. Weather, system down, poor network) · Defect must be fixed in order to continue testing. · Not enough testers. · Users take longer than expected. · Some users are not filing defects as they test.
Progress aligned as planned	Are they testing what they are supposed to test? **Time taken to test a case may differ depending on the test scenario and when testers plan their schedule, it may not be as simple as to just spread equal number of test cases per day throughout the phase. Sometimes progress rate could be ahead of plan because testers are conducting simple basic*

	test only. For example, time window to test bank interest rate calculation should be longer than test cases for basic customer information entry. PMO must remind the team to balance out time taken for testing instead of just number of cases.

Defect Status

All defects are bad and it is best to deliver final output in spotless state. However, in most projects this is very hard to accomplish due to endless manifestation of hidden defects. While the project team pushes beyond their limit to fix issues, PMO must find strategic approach to have the project proceed to the next level. There are two main areas PMO must work on.

1. Prioritization of defects to fix

People have different algorithm for fixing defects. Some people apply FIFO (First in, first out), some fix latest defects first, some fix set of easy ones first then move to complex ones and vice versa. PMO may not be able to fix defects on behalf or persuade testers to erase defects already logged in, but we can prioritize the defect list to avoid project entering red signal zone with risk of postponing transition schedule. Having a clear priority will allow the team to fully focus on closing items one by one as listed, instead of being interfered by different testers demanding to fix defects that each of themselves consider is most important.

2. Categorization of defects

So how do we prioritize defect list for the project team? Some clients refuse to accept transition unless all issues are closed but it is unwise to delay transition forever when the project is running out of time and budget. PMO must negotiate with client on condition for transition approval during test planning stage. Best way to do this, is to categorize defects into severity and impact to actual operation after transition. Following table is the sample defect status table.

Sample: Defect Status Table

Defect ID	Defect Description	Defect Type	Severity on tracker	Impact on business	Complexity of fix
149	Absence of detailed product validation checks in illustration	Validation rule issue	S2-Severe	High	Medium
440, 442	Mapping incorrect illustration table column in chart	Value mapping issue	S2-Severe	High	Very low
441	Refresh premium field and display blank when user changes SA or policy term	UI Presentation Issue	S3-Major	None	Very low
443	Table column width inconsistency	UI Presentation Issue	S2-Severe	None	High
444	PDF dynamic field value mis-mapping in Chinese version PDF	Value mis-mapping issue	S3-Major	High	Very low
445	Display # for negative values	UI Presentation Issue	S3-Major	None	Very low

Common mistake made by people is that they treat severity level and actual impact on business as the same. While severity is rated based on functional perspective, impact on business should be rated based on operational feasibility. For example, you are building a user sign-up page in a web site. Tester finds that if you enter more than 100 characters in first name field, the browser would immediately shut down. This shall be rated S1 since the system no longer functions when 100 characters are entered. However, impact to business may not be as high since the chances are slim for users to enter 100 characters for their name. When it comes to negotiating priority, relevant stakeholders must be present to give opinion and come to an agreement.

Defect Burn Rate

This data will tell us how well the project team is closing open issues. The best way to view this data is to create an overlapping chart for total number of defects versus total number of closed defects. Below chart is an example of defect burn rate chart.

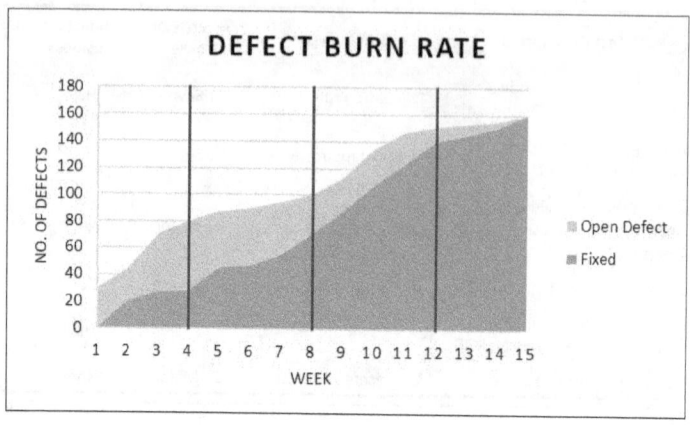

The dark gray shaded area indicates total number of closed defects over time and the light gray shaded area indicates total number of open defects over time. At the end, we want the border of two areas to meet. There are two things PMO must enforce. First, PMO must place regular checkpoints to identify gap between open and closed defects. If the gap goes over the threshold, PMO should wave yellow or red flag to the team. Second, PMO should gather both the project team and testers to determine root cause of slow progress and drive the team to come up with strategic plan rather than struggling to make a move with tones of defects squashing them down. Low defect burn rate doesn't mean your project team is being lazy or incompetent. I've seen many clients torturing engineers every hour to get a progress update. It's only going to make things worse by consuming engineer's time on having to deal with attacks from client.

Questions that should be addressed are:

✓ *Can we close majority of defect by fixing a specific issue?*
✓ *Are there defects originated from scenario outside planned test case?*
✓ *Is the retest being done in timely manner?*
✓ *What are the supports needed to catch up on schedule? Etc.*

It is critical to observe test progress in concurrent manner. Sometimes the defect burn rate may look bright at the beginning of test phase because the testers aren't testing many cases and this implies there is a high chance that defects will flood in towards the end of the test phase, which is a huge risk for the team. It is safer to have low defect burn rate in the beginning and gradually increase the rate towards the end.

Defect Reopen Rate

As much it is important to fix defects at a fast pace, it is critical to do a good fix so it doesn't return with 'reopen' label. What is even worse is impacting other test cases that had no issue in initial test round. Similar to defect burn rate, job of PMO is to guide the team to determine threshold for reopen defect number and wave yellow/red flag if the number shoots above the limit. For example, the project team could set 10% as tolerable level, 10%~20% as yellow flag and anything above that shall set the status to red and the team should be alarmed. PMO should also make sure project team does not receive full blame for high reopen rate. Questions that should be addressed are:

✓ *Is the same issue being rejected over and over? Or is the problem fixed in one area but causing problem in another area?*
✓ *Is the team doing enough analysis on other related parts before fixing defect?*
✓ *Are the details of problem being clearly communicated?*
✓ *Is the retesting done in using same scenario?*

9.6 Data to be Collected in Test Report

Nowadays most project teams are equipped with advanced test reporting tools and there is no need to manually create spreadsheet or struggle to combine different report templates sent by different teams. Since we don't want our project team to spend half their time making report data entry, we must select mandatory data to be entered. This could vary depending on the type of project you are conducting. Following is the most standard table used for projects to be able to illustrate test progress rates discussed in above sections.

Sample: Test Progress Tracking Table

Test Area	Plan	Actual	Pass	Fail	Reopen	Complete (%)	Pass (%)	Fail (%)	Reopen (%)
Function A									
Function B									

- Plan – Total number of test cases in the test plan
- Actual – Total number of test cases executed
- Pass – Total number of cases closed
- Fail – Total number of defects
- Reopen – Total number of defects reopened.

  **The definition of "Reopen" may vary from one individual to another. Some may never use the term reopen and some may label defects as "Reopen" when a fix made to a defect causes other problems. There should be an agreed standard among project team and testers. When the defect is at the peak and everyone is rushing off their feet for fixing and retesting, it is anticipated that people will ignore agreed standard and log defects based on their habit. However, it is still strongly recommended to agree on definition of defect status and encourage people to follow the guideline. We wouldn't remove road safety signs because people might not obey them, would we?

It is easy for PMO to become less involved in the project as we are not the ones to plan or execute test. However, PMO should closely monitor overall progress and provide following guidelines to the team:
- to ensure things are ready on the day 1 of testing.
- to write a test plan that can be used to track progress.
- to log relative test result data to identify current status in terms of progress rate.
- to mutually agree on grading defect severity to help prioritize defects.
- to analyze root cause on progress of testing/fixing.
- to negotiate fix/no fix cases based on severity.
- to govern scope creep during test phase by separating change request from defect.

10 TRANSITION PHASE

After running and confirming all test cases, now it is time to transfer work to the client or prospective users. Focus of PMO should be mainly on conducting change management with the project team. In this chapter, we will study steps taken for transition and change management in detail.

Entry Criteria	All test had been completed by both project team, client and testing organization.
Tasks for PMO	Guide the team to follow transition process on Operational Readiness Review (ORR). Supervise and lead change management.
Tasks for Project Team	Plan and execute ORR. Train operation team and provide user manual.
Exit Criteria	ORR condition satisfied and sign-off. All project deliverables transferred to the client.
Output Document	User manual. Maintenance plan.

10.1 High Level Flow

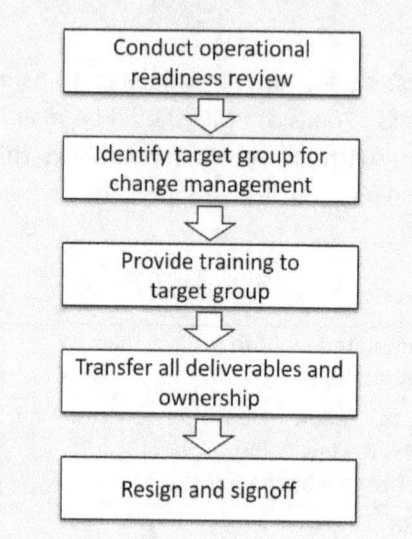

10.2 Steps for Transition

1) Plan Transition: Timeline, R&R, contacts for all relevant team/individuals, set Key Performance Parameters (KPP), training schedule. Transition plan should breakdown tasks into sub-dividable parts so it is easy to detect where the problem began and up to what extent rollback should be done when unexpected error occurs. For a system transition which takes less than a day, the plan could be partitioned based on activity for each hour. For complex, long term transition, plan can be produced by parts or functions.

2) Conduct Operational Readiness Review (ORR): Verify if the system, equipment, property, product is ready to be used. After transitioning of final output, operational readiness review must be verified even if the test cases had all been passed. Especially for IT projects where development environment is different to production environment, this is a critical step. Prospective users must check mandatory items for operation and grant approval for transition sign-off. KPP and

project completion criteria is defined during planning and updated throughout the project based on findings and discussions. Areas that should be closely examined includes:

- If the output delivered from the project is operable from Day 1 after the transition.
- Readiness of maintenance, operation resources and users. (i.e. training, manual etc.)
- KPP assessment on operational facility, systems, and equipment tests.
- Readiness to interface with existing operations.
- Certification/Permits/License required for initial operation.

3) Transfer and Resign: Submit all documentation and clear remaining work. Release resource and return facilities, equipment, systems. Surrender ownership of intellectual properties, terminate access rights from externals etc.

4) Signoff and setup team for post project review.

10.3 Change Management in Project

Change Management (CM) is a structured approach to implement changes to current environment (e.g. methodology, process, system, policy etc.) throughout organization/teams/individuals. Initiatives for change includes:

- Implementation of new project methodology.
- Customer expectation for better, faster and cheaper products.
- Change of organizational structure.
- New company operation strategy. (E.g. Accomplish 5% cost saving by cutting down negotiable expenses.)
- Introduction of enhanced technology. (E.g. From manual operation to automation.)
- Revised government regulation/policy.

- Change of project environment. (E.g. Working with virtual teams in overseas)

Change management is not a single event but it is continuously required throughout the project lifecycle and executed as required by project circumstances. Following figure indicates change management required throughout the project.

Change Management in Project Lifecycle

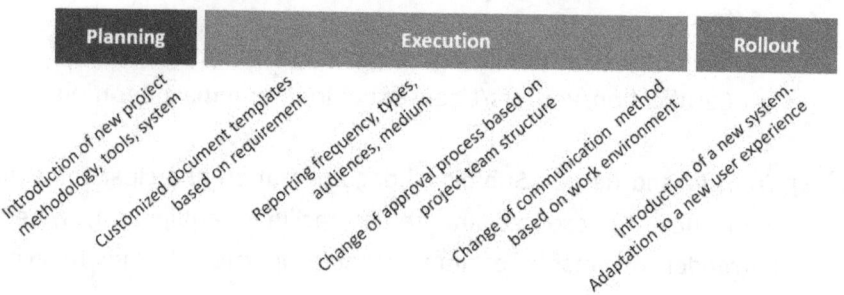

10.4 Barriers to Changes

- **Resistance to change by individuals/team**

  Most critical barrier to change management is resistance of individuals and teams. Unlike system change, which is quite straight forward in a way that we achieve certain level of output based on investments made, human resources have many variable factors. Depending on their role, level of impact due to change, personal attitude etc., they can be self-motivated to accept change (which scarcely is the case), or they can be a tough nut to crack. For example, let's say your company plans to locate a robot cleaner in every floor of your office so it is always on standby to clean dusty area. Most employees will be neutral about it, whereas the building maintenance team, especially the cleaning staffs, will be totally resistant since their job could be at stake.

- **Limitation of existing system**

  Changes may not be viable due to insufficient system support. For example, a company with subsidiaries running business worldwide is targeting to use common platform across all offices. Some of them may not be equipped with system capable to operate common platform and it maybe superfluous to replace/upgrade entire system, just to achieve global initiative.

- **Lack of executive support**

Most people tend to stay in comfort zone and it is very hard to talk them into accepting changes. Here, a single determined statement from executive is what the team needs. Without senior management support, it is very difficult to rollout change even with million good reasons since people won't pay attention.

- **Unrealistic expectations**

We've heard a lot say, "People fail to lose weight because they aim too high.". Well, same concept applies in change management. People expects too much in return for small adjustments they make. Ultimate goal of change management is to make improvement and bring business to a whole new level, but it's not going to be like turning pumpkin into a carriage with a stroke of magic stick. Setting an unrealistic expectation will only lower possibility to successful execution of change management. For example, a new project methodology applied with objective of preventing frequently occurred issues may reduce redundant time spent on solving repeated issues. However, this doesn't mean project will accelerate and hit the destination one months earlier than what had been planned originally.

- **Inadequate skills**

Skillset of team/individual is another barrier. Although people are willing to accept changes, they might not have the skill to manage operation after the change. For example, your head quarter decided to integrate email system of all regional offices and have everyone use common email application which only supports German. For non-German speaking country, it is unfeasible to apply this change due to language barrier.

- **Prohibited by uncontrollable factors (Weather, Regulation etc.)**

Sometimes change cannot be implemented due to factors that are beyond our control. For example, you are building an apartment complex in five different countries. Use of standardized equipment and machine may not be possible due to different weather condition. Consolidated management of tenants may be illegal by country regulation protecting personal information of residents outside the country.

10.5 Solution to Overcome Resistance

- **Motivate change by revealing current issue and positive solution from applying the change**

  You need to start from the group that is most influenced by current ongoing problem. Those who are willing to accept changes if it can resolve current issues. Although everything comes from facts and you must have objective view, you should speak with persuasive tone. Let them know you understand their pain points and this is the kind of change they need to accept in order to make things better. If they are unaware of potential problem, give them example cases they can relate themselves with.

- **Create vision for change by highlighting benefits to organization/team/individuals**

  It is harder to persuade people when change is required without having critical issues to solve. (i.e. Substantial benefit cannot be achieved right away.) For long term change management, you need to create vision and highlight benefits to organization/team/individuals. This cannot be done solely by your own story telling skill. You will need to search and analyze many case studies and best practices in the field and encourage the team to participate. For example, your company is planning to set Friday lunch as a regular team lunch to promote team engagement. This may be considered as an unnecessary activity to most team members. Some people may even take it as company intruding staff's personal lunch hour. In this case, you will want to share public survey result that highlights weekly team lunch can improve team building, co-worker relationship and communication with managers, which will lead to productive work hour. Never give them the impression that they are being forced to accept change for nothing.

- **Close management of transition to change by providing required support and recognition (E.g. Rewards on participation effort.)**
This solution is often used in introducing changes to individuals that are hard to monitor in close distance. Most common example is introducing new sales approach to sales agents. Since they work in more flexible environment to face customers in front end line, it is not easy to track how well they are applying changes into their everyday business. In this kind of situation, rewards and recognition will have people make their move out of their self-will.

- **Sustain momentum to boost and stabilize the change through continuous feedback exchange**
What is more important than implementing a change is, maintaining the flow. Sometimes change can be easily adapted by executive level pushing the team, by providing attractive rewards, or by the fact that change can temporarily remove their pain point. However, it is nature of human to go back to what they used to be, once things start to settle down. It is very important to keep the momentum flow and also do continuous feedback exchange to remind people that whatever changes had been made should be permanent. You should also leverage positive groups to encourage resistant groups by sharing benefits they have experienced.

- **Utilize political influence by developing executive support**
One word from the right authority can move the entire group. And frankly speaking, this is the fastest way to get things started. It is indeed vital to take close monitoring to the change process and continuously share benefits. However, political influence must be present to have everyone set their foot on change management.

10.6 Change Management Process

What to change?

To whom and how?

Take action!

Monitor and improve

Phase	Work Description
Prepare	Understand the baseline of current state and the need to change. Set the goal for the change.
Design	Identify parties impacted and possible resistance. Understand environmental change readiness. Decide how to approach each target. Create change management plan.
Execute	Execute change management plan.
Sustain	Observe and provide support to maintain the change. Gather feedback and make improvement on CM process.

10.7 Case Study – Global Project Reporting (GPR) System Rollout

Your company has signed a global contract to work with clients, partners and subcontractors all around the world. In order to establish consistent process, the project team needs to use GPR system for all communication, approval request and reporting. Only English can be processed by the system. How would you plan your change management?

  i. *Categorize target groups.*
 ii. *Identify level of resistance from each category.*
iii. *What would be the kind of support you will get from each group?*
iv. *What would be the kind of resistance you will get from each group?*
 v. *How would you resolve the issue?*

Case Study: Change of Communication Process and Tools

Target Group	Resistance Level/ Factors	Approach
Executive Members	**Moderate.** •Not a fast adaptor to new technology. •Prefer communication by face to face, hard copy document and manual signing.	**Dedicated Support.** ✓1:1 training by technical staffs. ✓Accompany verbal explanation in early stage of implementation.
Senior Supervisors	**High.** •Considers online reporting and communication as an additional task. •Stubborn to make changes to the work routine. •Not everyone is equipped with language ability to communicate in English.	**Political Influence and Pressure.** ✓Request the Project Sponsor to announce GPR as the official tool throughout the project. **Create Vision for Individuals.** ✓Emphasize emerging needs for global communication capability and let the individuals consider this as an opportunity.
Juniors	**Very Low.** •Majority prefers to use online system since the templates are fixed. •Flexible access to system will allow them to communicate faster.	**Training and Involvement.** ✓Provide training to learn flow of project communication and reporting. ✓Involve junior members in change management activities to guide the team to setup account and use the tool.

11 POST PROJECT REVIEW

Post project review is the final stage of the project, where project members and stakeholders gather and do a review on how project was executed. Ultimate purpose of this session is to determine lessons learned throughout the project journey and apply them to future projects to prevent repetition of same mistakes and make improvements.

Entry Criteria	All deliverables are submitted. Transition to operation completed. Client/User signoff on transition.
Tasks for PMO	Arrange and facilitate post project review session. Archive project close report for future. reference and process enhancement.
Tasks for Project Team	Participate in PPR meeting. Submit project closure report.
Exit Criteria	Project close report accepted and signed-off. Announce official completion of project.
Output Document	Lessons learned document.

11.1 High Level Flow

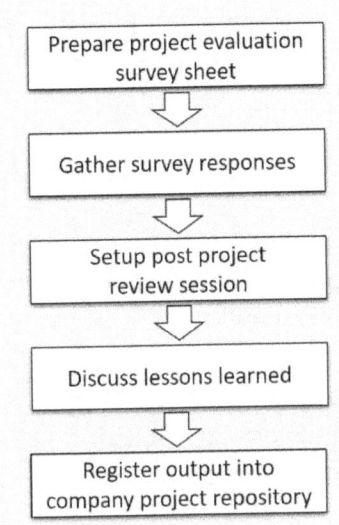

11.2 Purpose of Post Project Review

Post project review is a good opportunity to find remedies for weak area and to promote bright area into best practice for future performance enhancement. Post project review:

- Involves the project team and major stakeholders meeting together and reviewing what went well and what went badly during the project.
- Shares summary of project performance based on facts. (Scope delivery, time, cost)
- Measures success based on level of satisfaction between different stakeholders.
- Identifies areas for improvements and ways to improve them.
- Helps participants make the right decisions and plans so that the next project runs better.
- Helps clear up misunderstandings and other issues.

11.3 Preparation for PPR

By the time you are conducting PPR, all official task will have been completed and level of dedication from project team and stakeholders dramatically drain out. Thus, it is very difficult to draw active participation during PPR unless you prepare well. In order to have productive PPR session, following information must be gathered in advance.

- Project results.
- Schedule performance.
- Resource expenditures.
- Problems that arose during the project.
- Changes made in project objectives, schedules, and budgets.
- Unanticipated occurrences or changes in the environment during the project.
- Customers' satisfaction with the project results.
- Management's satisfaction with the project results.
- Effectiveness of the project-management processes.
- Lessons learned.

To gather above data, it is recommended that PMO circulate a survey to key stakeholders in advance to the session, so people have enough time to look back and review project performance from various aspects.

Sample: Project Evaluation Survey

Category	Questionnaire	Score
Scope and Services	Project met owner's requirements	
	Were the plans neat, thorough and technically correct?	
	Was the project scope under control throughout the project?	
Schedule	Was project completed on schedule?	
	Was the original schedule appropriate?	
Budget	Was project completed within expected budgetary constraints?	
	Was the profit target met?	
Project Team	Were staff skills adequate for project requirements?	
	Was there excessive overtime on this project?	
	Did consultants perform to expectations?	
	Was the contractor's performance adequate?	
	How well was the project team on track throughout the project?	
	Were there any difficulties in managing the client?	
	Were there any difficulties in managing the consultants?	
General Management	Were there any difficulties in marketing?	
	Were there any difficulties in project planning?	
	How effective was information flow and communications with client?	
Satisfaction	How satisfied are you with results delivered?	
Comments	*Recommendation for future projects*	

11.4 Important Tips on Preparation

· Give notification of PPR in advance

Circulate draft agenda, materials, and all expected attendees at least one week before the meeting. This advance notice gives people time to prepare for the meeting.

· Invite the right people

Invite key stakeholders of the project. If the list of potential invitees is too long, consider meeting separately with selected subgroups and then holding a general session in which everyone reviews results of smaller meetings then solicit final comments and suggestions.

· Lead session to be a learning experience rather than a finger-pointing session

As the project manager, you run the post-project evaluation meeting. At its outset, you need to declare that the session is a time for self-examination and suggestions for ensuring the success of future projects.

· Encourage people

Encourage people to identify what other people did well and to examine their own performance and see how they could've handled situations differently.

· Consider holding the session away from your office

People often feel more comfortable to do open discussion away from office. This can motivate discussion of new approaches when they're away from everyday work environments.

· Assign a note taker

Be sure to assign a person to take notes during the post-project evaluation meeting. Notes should list all the agreed-on activities to implement the lessons learned from the meeting and the people responsible for those activities.

11.5 Session Agenda

Depending on characteristics of project and company culture, post project review agenda may be different. Below is the most standard agenda you can use as a start to plan your session.

Sample: PPR Session Agenda

- Statement of the meeting's purpose.
- Specific meeting outcomes to be accomplished.
- Highlights of project performance, including the following:
  - *Results, schedules, and resources.*
  - *Approaches to project planning.*
  - *Project-tracking systems and procedures.*
  - *Project communications.*
  - *Project team practices and effectiveness.*
- Recognition and discussion of special achievements.
- Review of customer and management reactions to the project.
- Discussion of problems and issues.
- Discussion of how to reflect experiences from this project in future efforts.

11.6 Recommended Order of Discussion

1 Run through project performance based on factual data.
e.g. Scope delivery, schedule alignment, cost expenditure.

2 Identify items that went well and that could improve.
e.g. Approval requests were processed on agreed time, Documentation was not ready on time.

3 Identify items that are broken.
e.g. Daily progress meeting during build phase due to unavailability of participants, Monthly progress simulation.

4 Decide action plans.
File lessons learned and recommendations.

It is best to start with factual data walkthrough where no one has to disagree or argue. Sharing of data will also give opportunity for stakeholders to do a quick examination of overall performance. We then move to positive commenting. Things that went well and things that can improve. Recognizing team's effort will smooth overall tone and atmosphere of the meeting before going into discussion for negative area. As mentioned in earlier section, be mindful not to let anyone make personal attack in commenting on area that didn't go well. And finally, the documentation. It is not worth doing a PPR if there will be no lessons learned document to shelf on project repository. Make sure to produce document using company standard format.

CONCLUSION

Roles and responsibility of PMO is expanding bigger and bigger every day. As more technologies and systems are invented, operation and job around our business will have higher dependency on processes and at the end, it is all about defining and adhering to standards that is more promising.

Although this book provides efficient and effective manual for project level PMO, you will need to continuously seek for better ways to work around projects. Remember, what worked as the best standard may not always be, as our environment revolving around us changes.

I hope this book will be used as a good guideline and reference for your projects and make changes to your work. Thank you.

ABOUT THE AUTHOR

Jay is a professional global PMO. She has worked with many global clients, partners and affiliates all over the world for the past 15 years.
She is passionate about sharing her global experience and knowledge with project teams and individuals with vision to accomplish better project environment. She had successfully published online training and book on how to communicate with virtual teams via conference call. Although Jay had initiated her career in IT field, her courses are being promoted in construction industry with high reputation for training key essential skillset in project management.

Other works of the author:

· Effectively Managing Communication with Virtual Team
  - eBook edition: *www.amazon.com*
  - Video training edition: *www.udemy.com*

· Project Email Tool - *www.emailfactory.biz*